For we stand on the should

Disclaimer

Security—like life—is all about risk management, and there is no magic bullet or set of recipes to achieve absolute security. For that reason, we need to add a typical warning and disclaimer – this guide will help you, but of course, we can't take responsibility for what you do or don't do, or what your results may be. We live in a complex world, and computers and the Internet are near the top of that list when it comes to complexity and unpredictability.

Table of Contents

Preface

Website and cloud service security breaches have become increasingly more common in the news over recent years as even the largest of companies have suffered hacking incursions and lost customer data, i.e. your usernames, your passwords, your address, your credit card numbers, *your* data.

By way of example, in December of 2010, Gawker Media was compromised and 1.4 million registered usernames and passwords were stolen and shared on the Internet. Gawker Media includes popular websites such as Lifehacker, Gizmodo, and Gawker. While the Gawker Media sites do not take credit cards or collect enough personal information to be bound by strict regulations, the credentials stolen from Gawker Media provide valuable information that could be leveraged to access their users' more sensitive data elsewhere on the Internet.

If you worry that your credentials could be in the next security breach, you are absolutely justified. This easy-to-understand guide will arm you with the actions you need to take now to greatly strengthen your passwords and how you approach password security while reducing your risk and exposure.

This book contains over a dozen chapters each of which contains concrete steps that you should take along with detailed discussions of how and why.

These are the secret weapons that your computer- and security-savvy friends use and dole out to you in bits and pieces, all bundled into one accessible book.

Khalid J Hosein & Doug Felteau, Atlanta, GA, November 2014

About the Authors

The authors have almost 40 man-years of experience in IT, including having worked in computer security departments at Fortune 100 companies, and at the world's largest security software vendor, Symantec, as security consultants. They both hold the CISSP information security certification as well as an assortment of other IT and infosec certifications.

We welcome your comments and feedback. Contact:
Twitter: @kjhosein, @dfelteau
Web: http://www.GizmosForGeeks.com

How To Use This Book

This book does not have to be read in order to benefit from its advice; feel free to skip around to your heart's content. However, if you are in the least bit unfamiliar with the subject of security, we recommend that you read it all. It's not that long.

Most chapters contain actionable advice, and we recommend that you take those actions before moving onto another chapter. Some actions—changing your passwords for example—will take some time, so you should make a note for yourself to continue working on that while you move onto new chapters.

Each chapter will be divided into 2 main parts, what to do (action) and an in-depth discussion of why this works and/or is important.

We will start with the ground rules on handling your passwords and how to construct an appropriate password, cover little-known and rarely-used techniques for further obscuring your online presence, and delve into more advanced topics such as VPNs.

1. The Basics of Password Handling

Before we delve into anything too detailed, we'll start with the basics of handling passwords. Some of the items below will require more in-depth coverage that we will cover in later chapters, while some are simple enough to stand on their own. Don't be offended that some of these seem much too trivial to even mention; we want to be thorough. Incidentally, you would be surprised by what information security professionals encounter on a regular basis that passes for adequate password hygiene and management.

✓ Make your password *complex*. We'll cover what *complexity* really entails in the next chapter.

✓ Don't write your password down on pieces of paper, especially little yellow ones that you stick on your monitor!
  The exception *might* be if you've only written piece of it down and/or scrambled it in a way that only you know. Better still, use a *password manager*.

✓ Don't tell other people your passwords.

✓ Don't tell other people how you construct your passwords. For example, if you have a certain base around which you create all of them.

✓ Don't send your passwords via email. Ever.

✓ Don't type your password into websites that are not secured by SSL (Secure Sockets Layer) — look for the lock icon in your web browser.

If any of this sounds new to you or you think you may forget it occasionally, we strongly recommend printing it out and affixing it near your computer or monitor, copying it and putting it into a recurring calendar event, or automatically sending it to yourself via email periodically. Anything to help make it second-nature.

2. Password Complexity

Here's where we really dive into more detailed guidance. It is also at this point where you need to start taking action.

If you've ever been required to include numbers or symbols or uppercase letters, some combination of those and/or a minimum length, then you've already been exposed to *password complexity.*

If you don't have *multi-factor authentication* (which we'll talk about in a later chapter), then password complexity is your **best line of defense** against crackers[1].

Actions to Take

Choose passwords that are as long as the website or software application will allow[2], and that have at least *one of each* of these:

✓ numbers

✓ lowercase letters

✓ uppercase letters

✓ and symbols

---

1 We prefer to use the term *cracker* instead of *hacker* for people who use their computer skills for malicious, illegal or negative reasons. We still feel the title *hacker* is a badge of honor.

2 If you'd really like to pick a set length (that you can use as a preset in your password manager), 20 characters is currently quite reasonable.

The sequence should be random, i.e. don't use any dictionary words. This is one of those cases where a computer can do a better job than your brain so we highly recommend letting a password generator do it for you.

Detailed Discussion

A common way for attackers to figure out what your password is (i.e. crack it) is to use what's called a *dictionary*. No, this is not a traditional dictionary you're used to with words and definitions, but just lists of words, phrases, common misspellings, slang, celebrity names, pop culture references, common first and last names and many more fragments that people tend to use in their passwords.

Using a dictionary dramatically reduces the amount of time it takes to crack passwords, because they don't have to *brute force* the combinations, i.e. try every possible permutation of every single character. This is why it's important to force them to work as hard as possible, and if they're *only* using dictionaries, they're not going to crack your password.

To get an idea of the power of both length and randomness when it comes to the estimated time it might take a cracker or a computer to brute force your password, take a look at GRC's Password Haystack web page[3].

---

3 https://www.grc.com/haystack.htm

Now that you know, no more passwords like 'monkey', ok?! Now get cracking (pardon the pun!) - start changing at least some of those bad passwords. Ok, we know you may have hundreds. Start with the most important ones.

3. Use a Password Manager

After the last chapter, we're sure you are now creating and using complex passwords. Well done! But now we know you have a new problem – how to securely store and manage them.

You can't write them down – you will probably end up with lots of typos, not to mention that is not safe. You will also have too many to manage manually since you will now have different passwords for each service or website.

Enter the *Password Manager*.

Actions to Take

Start using a 3rd-party password manager. We recommend avoiding the password managers built into web browsers.

We recommend using 1Password[4], LastPass[5] or KeePass[6] as each of these password managers includes the features mentioned below starting with industry-standard encryption and one master password.

---

4 https://agilebits.com/onepassword
5 https://lastpass.com/
6 http://www.keepass.info/

Detailed Discussion

You could maintain a text file or a spreadsheet of your usernames and corresponding passwords, but you would need to make sure this file is protected with strong encryption. While this is certainly possible to do yourself, the tools available today don't make it straightforward and easy for everyone to choose the best encryption. On the other hand, the primary mission of password managers is to secure their contents.

The second option is to use the password manager built into your web browser. However, we recommend against using this option. Drawbacks include questionable or weak security, possibility of drive-by hacking from visiting malicious websites, browsers tend to be always open allowing for physical access, and lack of synchronization across multiple devices.

A first-rate 3rd-party password manager, however, yields numerous benefits including:

One (1) Master Password — A Master Password is both used to encrypt your data and to password protect the database of passwords. No one can view your passwords or other information stored in the password manager without knowing this password.

Because this password is critical, make it extremely complex, long and unpredictable per our guidance in the previous chapter, then commit to memory. On the bright side, you can conceivably reduce the number of passwords you need to remember to just this one, as all of the other passwords will be safely stored within the manager.

Secure Your Passwords with Industry-Standard Encryption — Each of the password managers we recommend encrypt data using Advanced Encryption Standard (AES), the same state-of-the-art encryption algorithm used as the national standard by the United States federal government. The password managers use 128 bit keys, and according to the National Institute of Standards and Technology (NIST), it would take 149 trillion years to crack a 128-bit AES key[7].

Complex Password Generator — The password managers we recommend all include the ability to create complex passwords of random strings. You can adjust what types of characters are included (i.e. letters, digits, and symbols) as well as the length of the generated password (we recommend at least 17-20 characters or higher; even better, use the maximum length that the website will let you).

One-Click Login or Copy & Paste — A common feature for password managers is the ability to perform a one-click login for many Internet sites. In some cases you might need to copy and paste a password depending on the login mechanism of a site but the vast majority allow for the

---

7 http://www.nist.gov/public_affairs/releases/g01-111.cfm#AES

password manager to automatically fill it in. This saves you from having to write down, memorize or even type them in.

Automated Form Filling — They also typically include the capacity to automatically fill in credit card and address information when shopping or fill in contact information such as name and email address when creating a new account. Gone are the days when you search frantically for your wallet while working against the Ticketmaster clock to buy the latest concert tickets!

Synchronized Across Browsers and Devices — As people use more devices to access their Internet services, this feature is becoming increasingly standard, and even necessary, for password managers. It gives you the ability to access your up-to-date usernames and passwords from any supported platform, which typically includes Windows, MacOS, Linux, iOS and Android.

Securely Store Other Data — Password managers can also frequently securely store more than just usernames and passwords. You can store notes, software licenses, credit cards and other personal information for a quick recall.

Protection Against Phishing — Both 1Password and LastPass offer protection against entering your password into websites that look like the legitimate version but are in fact masquerading in an attempt to capture your username and password.

As you can see, the benefits of a good password manager are significant, and once you start using one, you won't look back.

One last note regarding the choice of password manager. Although it's free, KeePass does require some work to pick the right version for your system and to set up synchronization. 1Password and LastPass are simpler and faster to install and configure.

.

4. Change Your Passwords Periodically

Changing your passwords on a regular basis is hopefully advice you've seen or heard before.

Actions to Take

Change your passwords periodically. If they're for sites with sensitive and/or data that is very valuable to you, then at least every 6 months.

Accounts with sensitive data would be things like banks and other financial services, but it could also be your email account and even your Facebook account (e.g. you don't want someone being able to login and post as you). Make a list of these critical accounts and set a recurring reminder in your calendar.

Detailed Discussion

You may be wondering why you should change your passwords if you already have strong ones. Here are 3 reasons:

First, if someone did capture a *hashed* version of your password, they could spend the time to brute force it (guess it by manually trying every possible permutation). If on the chance that your password was cracked in less than the time it took for you to change it, then they would have access to your account.

Second, if an attacker got a hold of not just your hashed password, but an entire database of them for a particular site, *and* that site did not use good encryption methodologies and technologies, then it would make cracking all the passwords easier. Once they figure out a few, cracking the rest would be very fast and easy.

The third and most alarming reason is this: if an attacker did actually manage to figure out your password, but was laying low and not tipping their hand, but instead waiting for a 'right' time to make their move. If you were in the habit of changing your password regularly, then the moment you did so, you would lock them out and force them to have to restart the crack of your password from scratch. Hopefully the site in question would have improved their security since then, thus extending the timeframe for your account safety.

Incidentally, many password managers can help you determine which passwords are due to be changed by showing either the last change date for the record or even the password itself.

5. Two-Factor Authentication

Your password is but one form of authentication. So is your driver's license or when you verify your name and address with a company over the phone. Those are all different forms of authentication.

Two-factor authentication (sometimes abbreviated to 2FA) strengthens the process by introducing a 2nd-form of authentication.

Actions to Take

If you notice any of the services you're using offering 2-factor authentication, enable it. **Immediately**.

It's too good to pass up. Attackers now have to jump through many more hoops in order to gain access to your account. We're not saying it can't be done, but it's that much more harder, and typically requires *social engineering*. For good measure, you should also change your password at this time as well.

The big 3 websites in terms of users, Google, Facebook and Twitter all offer it, and given that you may very well use them for 3rd-party authentication to other sites, it makes it that much more important to strengthen your password with them.

There is also an excellent reference website at TwoFactorAuth.org that lists top websites and whether or not they support 2-factor authentication.

Detailed Discussion

As we discussed in previous chapters, given enough time, computing power, an attacker may be able to crack passwords in a stolen password database. However, if the account is further secured with 2FA, the attacker will not be able to login as you with *only* your username and password.

As a side note, you may be wondering why not 3 or 4 factors of authentication (generalized as multi-factor authentication)? Sure, that's possible and is implemented in a few places, but remember that security is in a constant battle with convenience and practicality. So if it takes too long to log into something that you use frequently, you're probably going to disable the secondary authentication methods out of frustration.

Also, while a second factor of authentication dramatically enhances the security of your account or to put it another way, significantly lowers the probability of being hacked, additional factors only marginally improve that security. So the law of diminishing returns kicks in and the ROI isn't worth effort.

There are some caveats to using 2FA that you should be

fully aware of. First, some applications, especially mobile ones, don't allow you to login using 2FA. However, this is a problem that is gradually fading away as more vendors build this functionality in.

Next, if you enable 2FA on a service such as a bank or PayPal you may lose connectivity from an aggregation service (e.g. Mint). Again, this is seeing wider support as security concerns increase.

Last and most important, have a contingency plan should you lose your 2nd-factor device or mechanism (e.g. your smartphone or token/fob). Most of the larger sites (i.e. Google, Twitter, etc.) already have ways for you to access your account in such an event by using things like backup codes, backup factors, etc. Learn what these are, and ensure you understand them fully.

6. "Security" Questions

Many websites now infamously use something called *security questions* as a form of 2-factor authentication. While this is a positive step forward by those companies, we're going to take it a step further and improve its benefit even more.

Actions to Take

Make up random, nonsensical or unrelated answers to the questions, then store them as notes in your password manager. Don't ever put the real answer to the questions.

So instead of putting "Rover" as the answer to "What is your dog's name?", put something like "Moon Shot 2014" or even just something random, and let your password manager do the remembering for you.

Detailed Discussion

Although you might think that an attacker may not know what street you grew up on as a kid, your mom's maiden name or the name of your dog, it can be socially engineered out of you, your friends and family or gleaned from online sources.

"Social engineering" is the euphemism given to what is typically wrangling information out of people by means of bribery, pretense, being wily, or other psychological manipulation.

You may be wondering why we're recommending this mechanism since we extolled the virtues of 2-factor authentication in an earlier installment of this series. First of all, we're not recommending it at all, as many websites already require their use; we're improving its effectiveness.

However, unlike one of those small hardware tokens or say your cell phone, this form of 2FA is not 'something you have' but rather another form of 'something you know'. 2FA's effectiveness is significantly boosted by using different vectors to secure your account.

Incidentally, the 3rd main 2FA vector is 'something you are' and is typically biometric, e.g. fingerprints, optical scans, voice recognition.

7. Randomize Usernames

In the previous chapter, we talked about divorcing your 'security' questions from reality to practically eliminate the ability of an attacker to take educated guesses. Well we can apply that same technique to your usernames too! After all, the websites and companies don't care what your username is.

Actions to Take

Make up random usernames for the various Internet services you use. At the very least do not use the same usernames for financial sites as you use for social networking sites.

Detailed Discussion

You may think this is an extreme step to take, but with all the breaches of website databases around the Net, your username is one of the pieces of information that is typically **not encrypted and/or hashed**. Once a site's database is breached, an attacker can easily extract your username and a hashed password.

If they are able to break the password (which would be significantly more difficult for them using our tips in this series), the attacker will then attempt to login using your username and hacked password on financial sites and other Internet sites. At a minimum, they now have your username and probably email address with which they can then use to attempt to log into other common sites.

While an attacker could mess with your reputation on social media sites, which you might feel is devastating, having your bank account drained because you reused usernames and passwords is *actually* devastating!

8. SSL

SSL standards for Secure Sockets Layer and provides a secure channel between a server and a client. While this could refer to a mail server and a mail client such as Outlook, we are primarily talking about using SSL between a web server and a web browser.

It is not hard to imagine what an attacker would do if they could **intercept and decrypt** all data between the web site and your web browser.

Actions to Take

Whenever you are about to enter information into a website, be it sensitive, confidential or personal information and especially credit card information, you should ensure that you have a proper SSL connection. This is critical if you are paying for an item on an e-commerce site or logging in to a website, particularly to a financial site.

Detailed Discussion

Have you ever wondered why the checkout areas of e-commerce shops and Internet banking sites use SSL? It is because Internet traffic is susceptible to an attack called *packet sniffing*. Think of this as a wiretap — basically the attacker can "listen" to any communication going over the wire.

Typically, data being sent between your web browser and a remote web server is sent in plain text, i.e. unencrypted. This means that if an attacker were to perform packet sniff that traffic, they would be able to read it almost as easily as if they were looking over your shoulder as you typed. SSL protects all of that data by encrypting the entire *channel*.

Here's a rough analogy to SSL from the real-world: imagine that you're sending a letter via snail mail to a friend, and instead of writing it in the language of your choice, you scrambled all the letters with a *key* or *cipher*. While that key may be something very simple like changing each letter to the letter next to it in the alphabet, today keys are much more complex. Regardless, the only one that can *decrypt* or *decipher* the letter is you or your friend the recipient. Even if someone intercepts the letter, it would take a great deal of computing power and an extremely long time to decipher the contents.

So how can you make sure SSL is enabled when you are about to enter data? There are two steps. First look at the URL in the address bar in your web browser, and verify it starts with "**https**" instead of "**http**". Note the 's' which stands for secure. This will verify that you are utilizing the correct protocol. Next, you should verify the certificate is valid. Most Internet browsers have an icon that looks like a padlock next to the URL. You can click on the icon to inspect the validity of the certificate by clicking Show

Certificate or looking in Certificate Information for a mention that the certificate is *valid*. Some Internet browsers combine this step for you. In Google Chrome for example, if the certificate is valid the lock icon and *https* part of the URL will turn green.

If you'd like to take your certificate-inspection to the next level, use a service such as SSL Labs[8] to audit any other website's SSL certificates and cipher suites. And if they have a low grade, report it to the website, particularly if they're a bank or other institution that has to manage sensitive personal information. In today's security-sensitive atmosphere, many times these companies will take action, and it costs them relatively little to fix.

A note to our more technically-savvy readers: yes, we are absolutely aware that the current technical standard is *TLS* (Transport Layer Security). However, SSL was the original incarnation and SSL/TLS is still widely referred to generically as SSL.

---

8 https://www.ssllabs.com/

9. VPNs, Virtual Private Networks

Do you hang out at your local coffee shop a lot? Then you should know that their WiFi is typically not encrypted, so that means your fellow coffee-drinkers can sniff your network traffic unless you are using SSL (see the previous chapter). However, currently only a subset of websites have SSL encryption for some or all of their web pages. The good news is that you can minimize your risk exposure by using something called a *Virtual Private Network (VPN)*.

Actions to Take

If you want to improve your personal privacy on WiFi or wired networks, use a VPN. You can either use a VPN service such as ProXPN[9] or Private Internet Access[10] or setup your own proxy at home using a free proxy such as Privoxy[11] or OpenVPN[12].

Detailed Discussion

A VPN, or Virtual Private Network, provides a secure and

---

9 http://proxpn.com/

10 https://www.privateinternetaccess.com/

11 http://www.privoxy.org/

12 http://openvpn.net/

private tunnel over another connection, usually a public connection such as the Internet. VPNs secure your computer's Internet connection by encrypting all the data you send and receive. This sounds similar to SSL but rather than encrypting the session from browser to web site, you are encrypting your connection to the *termination point* of the VPN.

Why is this important? If a web site has not implemented SSL your traffic can be sniffed by anyone else connected to the network. When you use a VPN, all of your traffic is encrypted prior to being sent and through the Internet, even for those web sites that do not have security implemented.

However, and this is important, it's not encrypted *all the way* to the end website, because the encryption goes from your computer to the VPN's termination or exit point. From this exit point to the target website or service, the traffic will typically be unencrypted, unless that target site uses SSL. Note that if a website does not support SSL, you (the user) can't force it.

Two additional benefits of using a VPN are that you gain a high degree of anonymity and, depending on the provider, you can even mask your location. So for example, you could appear to a UK website that you are within the UK although you're in another part of the world, as long as your exit point is in the UK.

When looking for a good VPN service, there are a few

factors you will want to consider:

Operating System Support – Will the VPN service support all your devices and operating systems? You will want a consistent experience across all your devices from your laptop to your phone to your tablet. The providers we recommend all provide guides or software to easily use their VPN services from any of your devices.

VPN Exit Points – Where does the VPN terminate or exit to the Internet and are there multiple points? If all your traffic is VPNed through Turkey, you might notice a considerable degradation when using the Internet, so pick a VPN vendor that provides multiple exit points in multiple countries, including at least one that's geographically close to you.

Logging Policies – While your data is secure over the local coffee shop's connection when using a VPN, the VPN provider could log all your data and either use that information or make it easier for the government to subpoena the information. Most reputable VPN services *do not* perform logging or perform minimal logging not related to what content you are viewing.

Price – Finally, consider what it costs. You get what you pay for, so if you are concerned about anonymity and security you will want to choose a for-fee provider versus a free VPN service. Free VPN services usually perform logging and require you to suffer through pop-up ads. The services we recommend cost roughly USD $7 to $10 a month.

10. Unsubscribe/Delete

An easy way to simplify both your life *and* your password management is to minimize.

Actions to Take

If you don't use a website or service any more, *delete* your account. But before you do, log in and change your password to something random.

Detailed Discussion

The fewer logins you have, the smaller your *footprint* and *exposure* on the Net. While we're not saying you should live in a cabin without an Internet connection (perish the thought!), it makes sense to get rid of things you don't use any more. Think of it as continuous spring cleaning.

As for why you might first change your password before deleting your account, consider this — what if the folks running the site (due to an oversight, software bug or other reason) don't entirely delete your account entry, and then some attackers get their database with your formerly weak password? At least if your password is strong and unique, this makes it practically impossible for someone to use that data against you somewhere else.

11. Don't Use Public or Friends' Computers

While you can certainly surf the Internet from a friend's computer or a public computer, such as a library computer, or at an Internet café, you should **never** enter your personal information on these public machines.

Actions to Take

Do not use a public or a friend's computer to access your online accounts. **Never** use a public machine to make online purchases or to check your bank account.

There are situations where it may be inevitable, for example if you are traveling without your own computer. In these situations you can use PortableApps[13], a freely available open-source application that allows you to run many popular applications including web browsers (e.g. Firefox and Chrome) from a USB thumb drive.

If you do not have PortableApps, you can still somewhat protect yourself by ensuring that you use Incognito or Private Browsing mode in the borrowed browser. At the very least you *should not* check the "Remember Me" option when logging in. Also, make sure you actually log out of any accounts when done and not just close the

---

13 http://portableapps.com/

browser. Additionally, when you finish clear the cookies, cache and temporary files in the browser.

Detailed Discussion

Using borrowed computers that you do not have control over has multiple hazards including: Web sessions left accidentally open, having your credentials stolen via a *keylogger*, leakage of your personal data onto the computer's local storage, and more. A simple example of this would be pulling up a popular website in a computer store's display model to find someone else is still logged into their account.

As described above, your best option if you must use a public machine is to use PortableApps or something similar. This option takes a little preparation and you need to carry a USB thumb drive with you but is fairly simple to setup. Incidentally, PortableApps.com comes with KeePass, one of the Password Managers we mentioned earlier in the series.

Now, if you do not have a Portable Apps USB drive, or forgot to bring it with you, you need to know how to properly clean a public machine when you are done using it. When sitting down at a public machine, before you do anything make sure you turn on Private Browsing. Private Browsing, called Incognito or InPrivate Browsing depending on the browser hides your online behavior *on the local computer* by not saving cookies or temporary Internet files/cache. Additionally, your browsing history, form data and saved passwords are not stored in your browser.

How to Start a Private Session in Chrome and in Firefox

Chrome: Open the browser and immediately click on the *Chrome menu* in the upper right hand corner. The Chrome menu is represented by the three lines on top of each other (the 'hamburger' icon). From the Chrome Menu choose *New incognito window*. You can also use *Control-Shift-N* in Windows or *Command-Shift-N* on a Mac.

Firefox: Open the browser and click *File* then select *New Private Window*. You can also click *Control-Shift-P* in Windows or *Command-Shift-P* on a Mac.

Additionally, you might consider deleting your cache and other browser data. You will definitely want to perform this if you did not use the Incognito or Private browsing option in the browser. This process will delete your browsing and download data, saved form data, cookies and Temporary Internet files.

How to clear your cache, etc. in Chrome and in Firefox

Chrome: Click on the *Chrome* menu, select *Tools* then select *Clear browsing data*. A dialog will appear, select the checkboxes for the types of information that you want to remove (we recommend all) and the menu at the top to choose the amount of data you want to delete then click *Clear browsing data.*

Firefox: From the Firefox menu bar, click on the *Firefox menu* then select *Preferences.* Select the *Advanced Panel,* click on the *Network* tab then click *Clear Now* in the *Cached Web Content* section.

Regardless of what browser you use, we also recommend disabling both the Java runtime and scripting (typically JavaScript). Unfortunately, many websites require JavaScript, but if you use a browser plugin/extension like NoScript[14] or ScriptSafe[15], you'll be able to granularly control which sites can run scripts.

---

14 https://addons.mozilla.org/En-us/firefox/addon/noscript/
15 http://goo.gl/ywhQlX

12. Sign up for BreachAlarm

If you've read everything to this point, you may very well be overwhelmed and possibly a little paranoid that some of your passwords have already been compromised. Don't be. At least not entirely. Better to take action than to worry. It's also good to take preventative action.

Actions to Take

Sign up for the free service offered by BreachAlarm[16] (formerly known as Should I Change My Password?) If you have multiple email addresses, enter those as well. If you get an alert, change any and all passwords for accounts you have listed in the disclosure **immediately**.

Detailed Discussion

BreachAlarm has a very large database of known email addresses tied to accounts that have known to have either been hacked or at least copied by crackers in their encrypted forms. In case you're wondering, they have this because crackers have an idiosyncratic habit of dumping these databases onto the Internet both as a show of force and as a way to shame the service provider for their poor security.

---

16 https://breachalarm.com/

What BreachAlarm does for you is twofold:

✓ They compare your email address to what's in their database and lets you know if there's a match.

✓ They keep track of hacking disclosures and alert you immediately via email if your email address matches something in one of the known database dumps.

You should immediately change passwords for accounts listed in any alerts.

13. Did your Password get Hacked?

If you either know or even believe that your password was hacked, here are some steps you should take, most of them immediately.

✓ If it's your email account, change the password, and enable 2-factor authentication if your email provider offers it. Even if it's not your email account, but you think the attacker may have some gained access, change the password.

✓ Check your Sent folder to see if there's anything suspicious in there. Sometimes, malware sends out email from your account to try to entrap your contacts as well.

✓ Run a full anti-virus (AV) scan of your computer. Good free options include AVG[17] and Avast[18]. Good premium options include Norton[19] and Kaspersky[20].

✓ Since no AV package is 'perfect', we recommend scanning with another standalone anti-malware program, such as the well-regarded Malwarebytes[21].

---

17 http://free.avg.com/
18 http://www.avast.com/
19 http://norton.com/
20 http://kaspersky.com/
21 http://www.malwarebytes.org/

If you're still worried, have your local computer geek (yes, that's a term of admiration!) take a closer look at your machine.

✓ If you have other very important accounts with the same email address and passwords, change those immediately as well.

✓ This is also a good time to change those usernames as well. We talked about this earlier in the chapter on randomizing your usernames.

✓ It's a good idea to check your credit cards and bank statements for suspicious charges and/or debits.

14. Closing Thoughts

Boom! We're all done and now you're an "Xpert"! But in all seriousness, if you've taken action on even half of our suggestions, based on our experience, you're better covered and prepared than most other folks out there.

But don't lose your sanity. Take proper precautions as we've laid them out, but don't worry yourself to death or obsess after that.

Passwords and security—like life—is a risk management game. Keep this in mind when you're considering your exposure. We don't live in villages of dozens or hundreds any more, but cities and countries of millions. You're a needle in a haystack and as sad as this may sound, you just may not be that interesting of a target. But in this case, that's a good thing!

Now change a few passwords and go enjoy the rest of what the Net has to offer.

www.ingramcontent.com/pod-product-compliance
Lightning Source LLC
Chambersburg PA
CBHW051216050326
40689CB00008B/1337